ALTERNATOR
BOOKS™

MAGNETISM

INVESTIGATIONS

KAREN LATCHANA KENNEY

Lerner Publications ◆ Minneapolis

To our future scientists and their unknown discoveries

Content consultant: Kevin Finerghty, adjunct professor of Geology at State University of New York, Oswego; Earth science teacher at Pulaski Academy and Central Schools, Pulaski, New York

Lerner Publications Company
A division of Lerner Publishing Group, Inc.
241 First Avenue North
Minneapolis, MN 55401 USA

For reading levels and more information, look up this title at www.lernerbooks.com.

Main body text set in Aptifer Slab Regular 11.5/18.
Typeface provided by Linotype AG.

Library of Congress Cataloging-in-Publication Data

Names: Kenney, Karen Latchana, author.
Title: Magnetism investigations / Karen Latchana Kenney.
Description: Minneapolis : Lerner Publications, [2018] | Series: Key
    questions in physical science | Audience: Ages 8–12. | Audience:
    Grades 4 to 6. | Includes bibliographical references and index.
Identifiers: LCCN 2016050831 (print) | LCCN 2016054382 (ebook) |
    ISBN 9781512440058 (lb : alk. paper) | ISBN 9781512449587 (eb pdf)
Subjects: LCSH: Magnetism—Juvenile literature. | Geomagnetism—
    Juvenile literature.
Classification: LCC QC757.5 .K457 2018 (print) | LCC QC757.5 (ebook) |
    DDC 538—dc23

LC record available at https://lccn.loc.gov/2016050831

Manufactured in the United States of America
1-42267-26124-3/20/2017

CONTENTS

FINDING THE WAY

You're hiking in the woods, and suddenly everything looks the same. You're lost, and there's no trail in sight. Thankfully, you've got your **compass**. You pull it out and hold it still. The needle swings around, showing you which way is north. Now you can find your way. Compasses are great tools, especially in the woods or open seas where there aren't many landmarks. Sailors have used compasses to navigate seas since the twelfth century. They always work, but do you know why? It has to do with magnets and magnetism. Magnets are pretty much everywhere, from the door

The needle of a compass always points north. People began using simple compasses for navigation even before they understood how magnetism worked.

of your fridge to the inside of your laptop. Have you ever wondered what makes magnets work? Or why some things stick to magnets and others don't? These are the kinds of questions that lead to scientific theories. Scientists study the world and ask questions about how it works. Then they test their ideas through experiments and come up with answers based on evidence. This process is known as scientific inquiry. Through questions and experiments, we can learn a lot about our world. What do you want to know about magnetism?

WHAT IS A MAGNET?

Have you ever made a magnetic paper clip chain? You just stick one paper clip to a magnet, and then you can stick a second paper clip to the first one. Soon you have a whole chain of dangling paper clips. But if you take away the magnet, all the paper clips fall apart.

How can the paper clips be magnetic one minute and then lose that force the next? And why does the magnet stay magnetic? Magnets have an invisible force that causes magnets to stick to some metals and to other magnets. This force can also make some metals into magnets for a short time.

Some of these paper clips stick to other paper clips, even though they are not touching the magnet. The paper clips have become temporary magnets.

Some ancient Chinese compasses were made from a flat piece of bronze and a magnetic stone carved into the shape of a spoon. The spoon would spin to point in a north-south direction.

EARLY MAGNETIC DISCOVERIES

One kind of magnet is a mineral called **magnetite**. Natural magnets are stones that contain magnetite. The ancient Greeks and Chinese were the first to know about these magnetic stones, which are called **lodestones**. They realized that the stones attracted iron. They also found out that if they rubbed a steel needle with a lodestone, the needle became magnetic too. If the needle was allowed to move freely, it pointed north. This discovery led to the first compass.

In the sixteenth century, English doctor William Gilbert tested lodestones. Gilbert knew several sailors and others who studied navigation. He knew that compasses were important. But he also saw that many people did not understand how compasses or magnetism worked. Gilbert wanted to learn more. He conducted several experiments using a metal needle and a round lodestone. In 1600, he published the first scientific study of magnetism, *De Magnete*. Through his experiments, Gilbert found that magnets attracted certain metals such as iron. Gilbert also tested early ideas about magnetism. One early scholar thought that a needle rubbed with diamonds would point north. Some people thought that garlic made lodestones weaker. Gilbert proved both of these theories wrong.

The most magnetic metals are iron, nickel, and cobalt. Nickel (*right*) is often combined with aluminum and cobalt to make magnets.

HARDWARE DISEASE

Understanding magnetic materials can be very helpful. Cows often accidentally eat nails or other bits of metal. This metal can become stuck, keeping the cow from digesting properly. It can also tear or poke holes in the cow's stomach or heart. Farmers use magnets to save their cows. They put bar-shaped magnets inside the cows' stomachs to attract the metal. To check whether the magnet is still in place, the farmer uses a compass.

CHAPTER 2

HOW DO MAGNETS WORK?

Have you ever tried to push two magnets together? Did you notice that if you held the magnets one way, they snapped together, but if you held them the other way, they wouldn't even touch?

French scholar Petrus Peregrinus studied lodestones in the late thirteenth century. He placed a needle on a round lodestone, then traced a line around the lodestone in the direction the needle pointed. He repeated this several times, placing the needle in

These kinds of magnets make it easy to observe and experiment with magnetic poles.

different places around the lodestone. Soon the lines all came together at two points on either end of the lodestone. Peregrinus noticed that the magnet seemed to be most powerful at the ends. He experimented and saw that the ends, which he called poles, acted in a certain way. These poles came to be known as the magnetic north and south poles. Two north poles (which are known as like poles) will push against each other, but a north and a south pole (known as unlike poles) pull together.

Peregrinus wrote about magnets while working as an engineer for the French army in 1269. Historians know little else about his life.

MAGNETIC PARTICLES

Why is magnetism so strong at the poles? It starts with a magnet's many atoms. Atoms are the basic parts of all matter. And each atom is made up of particles called protons, neutrons, and electrons. The electrons orbit around the protons and neutrons.

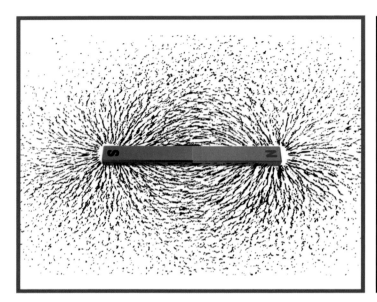

Tiny iron filings line up around a magnet, making it easy to see its magnetic field.

The spinning electrons cause an atom to have a **magnetic field**. So each atom is like a tiny magnet with its own north and south poles. This means that everything has magnetic force. Some things, such as wood or cloth, are weakly magnetic. Their atoms' magnetic fields stay separate from each other.

But in magnetic objects and magnets, atoms group together in **domains**. The domains all point toward a pole. This makes the atoms' magnetic fields join together, and the object becomes strongly magnetic. The magnetic field flows out of the pole and around the magnet. It moves back into the magnet at its opposite pole. This makes the object strongly magnetic at its poles.

MAGNETIC DOMAINS

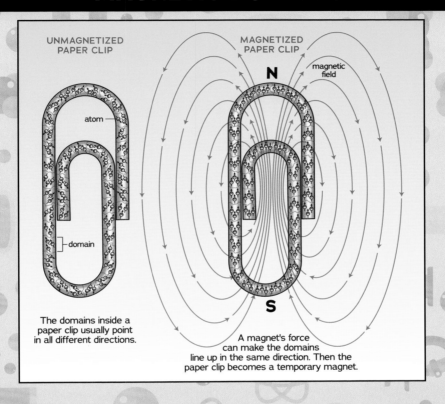

UNMAGNETIZED PAPER CLIP

atom

domain

The domains inside a paper clip usually point in all different directions.

MAGNETIZED PAPER CLIP

magnetic field

N

S

A magnet's force can make the domains line up in the same direction. Then the paper clip becomes a temporary magnet.

When you put a magnet near a magnetic object such as a paper clip, the magnetic field works through the paper clip. It makes the paper clip's domains line up too. This is why a paper clip can become a temporary magnet that pulls on other paper clips. When the magnet is removed, the domains in the paper clip no longer align, and the paper clip loses its power.

CHAPTER 3

HOW DO ANIMALS MIGRATE?

Immediately after they are born, baby sea turtles head to the water and swim hundreds of miles into the open seas. Then, after many years, they are ready to mate and lay eggs. So the adult sea turtles find their way back to the exact same beaches where they were born. Other animals such as birds, salmon, and monarch butterflies migrate great distances too. But how do they know where to go?

Monarch butterflies from eastern North America migrate to Mexico for the winter.

EARTH'S MAGNETIC FIELD

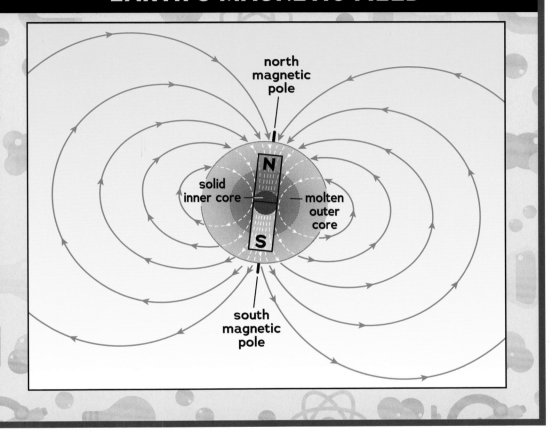

north magnetic pole

solid inner core

molten outer core

N

S

south magnetic pole

ONE BIG MAGNET

Through his experiments in the sixteenth century, William Gilbert concluded that Earth is one giant magnet. This is why a compass works. A magnetic compass needle is pulled by Earth's magnetic field to point in a north-south direction. Earth's core is divided into two layers. Scientists believe Earth's magnetism comes from the **molten** metal outer core, which surrounds a solid iron inner core at Earth's center. The liquid core moves and creates a magnetic field that exits Earth's South Pole, circles the planet, and then enters through the North Pole.

Just as a magnetic compass needle responds to Earth's magnetic field, scientists think that migrating animals can somehow sense Earth's magnetic field. This shows them where to go. It may have something to do with magnetite, which has been found inside animals including sea turtles and pigeons. Scientists have conducted several experiments to test the ability of pigeons and sea turtles to navigate.

A flock of snow geese flies north in spring. Some geese migrate more than 3,000 miles (4,828 kilometers).

DANCING LIGHTS

Earth's magnetic field protects Earth from **radiation** and particles in space. But particles from the sun can excite particles in the magnetic field. These particles break away from the field, go into the atmosphere, and move toward the magnetic poles. When these particles combine with gases in Earth's atmosphere, they create incredible colorful lights in the sky. The lights, known as aurora borealis and aurora australis, are often easiest to see in the winter in places such as Alaska and northwestern Canada.

These newly hatched sea turtles make their way from the beach into the ocean.

In one experiment, scientists attached magnets to the heads of a group of sea turtles. To another group, they attached nonmagnetic metal bars. The sea turtles with magnets took longer to navigate and followed less direct routes. It seems the magnets disrupted their ability to sense Earth's magnetic field. Scientists have many theories about sea turtle navigation, but they are still not sure exactly how sea turtles use magnetism to navigate. In 2012 scientists also found magnetic cells in rainbow trout. These cells rotated toward a magnetic source. It's a big step toward understanding *how* animals sense Earth's magnetic field.

SCIENCE IN PRACTICE

Scientists wanted to understand the magnetic cells in trout. So they took groups of cells from a trout's nose. They put these cells on a surface under a microscope. Then they moved a magnet around the surface to see if they could find which cells were magnetic. The scientists thought the magnetic cells would move in the direction of the magnet. They watched and saw that some of the cells moved. They were then able to remove these magnetic cells and study them further.

CHAPTER 4

WHAT MAKES AN ELECTRIC GUITAR'S SOUND?

Almost every time you listen to a popular song, you're hearing an electric guitar. Did you know that both magnets and electricity work together to make this instrument work? This is called electromagnetism.

MAKING CONNECTIONS

Early scientists thought of electricity and magnetism as two separate things. But Danish physics professor Hans Christian Ørsted found that electricity could make magnets move. This proved that electricity creates a magnetic field.

Electric guitars have a unique sound. You can probably recognize the sound—but do you know how it works?

SCIENCE IN PRACTICE

During a demonstration, Ørsted made an electrical circuit by connecting a battery and a wire. Then he made an incredible discovery. He noticed that the needle of a compass nearby moved from its north-pointing position. Instead, it pointed toward the wire. He experimented with electricity and magnets for the next three months. He tried different kinds of wires, and the compass always moved. It couldn't be stopped by shielding the compass with wood or glass either. Then, in 1820, he published his results— electricity makes a magnetic field.

Ørsted demonstrates electromagnetism to a crowd.

An electromagnet is a magnet made with electricity and a magnetic object. The magnetic field can be switched on and off by turning the electricity on or off. British electrical engineer William Sturgeon made the first strong electromagnet in 1825. He found that wrapping an electrified wire around a piece of iron magnetized the iron. American scientist Joseph Henry built upon Sturgeon's work, insulating his wires and wrapping them in layers around an iron core. It made a more powerful electromagnet.

Then scientists began to wonder if maybe magnets could make electricity too. In the 1830s, scientist Michael Faraday experimented with moving magnets. He moved a magnet in and out of a wire coil. The magnet made electricity in the coil.

When electricity moves through these wire coils, a magnetic field is created, magnetizing the core of the electromagnet.

The gold plate on this guitar covers its pickup. The strings move above the pickup to create a current.

This helps explain how an electric guitar works. Its pickup is a small part under the guitar's strings that converts the movement of the strings into electricity. The pickup is made of a magnet wrapped with wire. The magnet makes the guitar's metal strings magnetic. When the magnetic strings are plucked, they create an electrical current in the wire of the pickup. Then the electricity becomes the sound we can hear through the amplifier and speaker.

CHAPTER 5.

HOW DOES A MAGLEV TRAIN WORK?

Did you know some trains hover over their tracks? They are superfast and barely make a sound. These trains are known as maglev (magnetic levitation) trains, and they use magnetism to move along a track.

The first fully operating maglev train system opened in England in 1984. Construction on this Japanese maglev train began in 2015.

One kind of maglev train floats above its track because of the pushing power of magnets. Like poles on the track and the bottom of the train face each other. The powerful magnets repel, holding the train above the track.

Maglev trains have no engines. Instead, they move forward because of magnetic coils in the track's walls. These coils both pull and push the train forward using magnetism. The poles alternate between north and south along the walls. A south pole on the track wall pulls a north pole on the train's side. Right behind the wall's south pole is a north pole. It pushes against the train's north pole. Together, this pushing and pulling makes the train move forward.

Operators are testing this Japanese maglev train to figure out the best speed for a route between Tokyo and Nagoya, Japan. They hope to open the route in 2027.

MAGLEV MOTION

HOW A MAGLEV TRAIN FLOATS

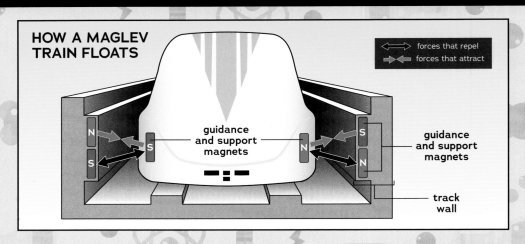

HOW A MAGLEV TRAIN MOVES

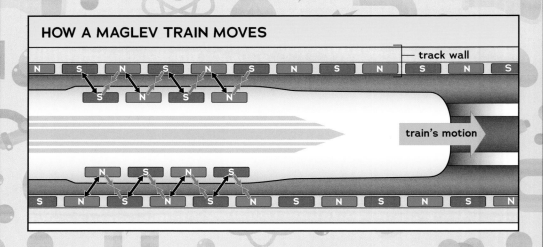

Because maglev trains don't touch the tracks, **friction** that could slow the trains down is not a problem. Instead, maglev trains can reach very high speeds—around 200 to 300 miles (322 to 483 km) per hour. In 2015 a Japanese maglev train broke a world speed record. It reached an incredible 375 miles (603 km) per hour.

EVEN MORE MAGNETS

Magnetism is a force that affects our entire planet. It guides animals during long migrations and helps produce the electricity we use every day. Scientists have studied how magnetism works and can be used. Their experiments, research, and results help us understand how magnetism affects our world. But there is still more to learn and discover. What questions do you have about magnets?

Do you want to see magnetism at work? Make your own electromagnet and see how an electric current creates a magnetic field.

❷ WHAT YOU'LL NEED

- wire strippers
- 4 feet (1.2 meters) of thin copper-coated wire
- 2 feet (0.6 m) of thin copper-coated wire
- a 3-inch (7.6-centimeter) nail
- tape
- a new D-size battery
- paper clips

❷ WHAT YOU'LL DO

1. Ask an adult for help using the wire strippers. Strip 1 inch (2.5 cm) of coating off the ends of both wires.
2. Wrap the 2-foot (0.6 m) wire around the nail. Start at one end of the nail, leaving the stripped end free. Wrap the wire in one direction toward the other end of the nail, leaving the other stripped end free.

3. Tape one stripped wire end to one end of the battery. Attach the other stripped wire end to the opposite end of the battery. That should magnetize the nail.
4. Hold the nail over a pile of paper clips. How many paper clips does it attract? What do you notice about your magnet? Record your results.
5. Try steps 1 to 3 with the longer piece of wire. Then hold the nail over the paper clips. Has anything changed? Does the magnet seem stronger or weaker? How many paper clips does it attract? Record your results.
6. When you are done with this experiment, disconnect the wire from the battery.

❷ FOLLOW-UP

Review the data from your experiment. Did the longer or shorter wire make a stronger magnet? Why might this be? Based on your results, what can you conclude about electromagnets?

compass: a tool for finding a direction using a magnetized needle that always points north

domain: a small, random region in a magnetic substance

friction: a slowing force on objects when they rub against each other

lodestone: a stone with iron in it that acts as a magnet

magnetic field: the area around a magnet or an electric coil that attracts magnetic metals such as iron or steel

magnetite: a black mineral that contains iron

molten: melted by very great heat

radiation: energy in the form of invisible rays or particles

LERNER

SOURCE

Expand learning beyond the printed book. Download free, complementary educational resources for this book from our website, www.lerneresource.com.

FURTHER INFORMATION

Arbuthnott, Gill. *Your Guide to Electricity and Magnetism*. New York: Crabtree, 2017.

BBC Bitesize: Magnets
http://www.bbc.co.uk/education/guides/zxxbkqt/revision

Discovery: Maglev Trains
http://www.discovery.com/tv-shows/other-shows/videos/extreme-engineering-season-1-shorts-maglev-train

ESA Kids: ESA's Swarm Prepares for Flight
https://www.esa.int/esaKIDSen/SEM7P5KX3XG_Earth_0.html

Loria, Laura. *What Is Magnetism?* New York: Britannica/Rosen, 2015.

Marsico, Katie. *Key Discoveries in Physical Science*. Minneapolis: Lerner Publications, 2015.

National High Magnetic Laboratory: Magnet Academy
https://nationalmaglab.org/education/magnet-academy

Walker, Sally M. *Investigating Magnetism*. Minneapolis: Lerner Publications, 2012.

INDEX

PHOTO ACKNOWLEDGMENTS

The images in this book are used with the permission of: design elements: © iStockphoto.com/kotoffei; iDesign/Shutterstock.com. © iStockphoto.com/MarkFGD, p. 4; © iStockphoto.com/Dean Mitchell, p. 5; © iStockphoto.com/Pat_Hastings, p. 6; World History Archive/Alamy Stock Photo, p. 7; Susan E. Degginger/Alamy Stock Photo, p. 8; Dick Kenny/Shutterstock.com, p. 9; design56/Shutterstock.com, p. 10; INTERFOTO/Alamy Stock Photo, p. 11; imagedb.com/Shutterstock.com, p. 12; © Laura Westlund/Independent Picture Service, pp. 13, 15, 26; JHVEPhoto/Shutterstock.com, p. 14; Delmas Lehman/Shutterstock.com, p. 16; Frozenmost/Shutterstock.com, p. 17; Kjersti Joergensen/Shutterstock.com, p. 18; © Phil McLean/Minden Pictures, p. 19; © iStockphoto.com/RapidEye, p. 20; Photo Researchers, Inc/Alamy Stock Photo, p. 21; wisawa222/Shutterstock.com, p. 22; Petr Malyshev/Shutterstock.com, p. 23; AP Photo/Kyodo, p. 24; YMZK-Photo/Shutterstock.com, p. 25.

Front cover: © iStockphoto.com/akwitps (pins); © iStockphoto.com/kotoffei (science items); iDesign/Shutterstock.com (question mark).